M000203885

George Washington Carver

AGRICULTURAL SCIENTIST

OTHER YOUNG YEARLINGS YOU WILL ENJOY

YEARLING BOOKS/YOUNG YEARLINGS/YEARLING CLASSICS are designed especially to entertain and enlighten young people. Patricia Reilly Giff, consultant to this series, received the bachelor's degree from Marymount College. She holds the master's degree in history from St. John's University, and a Professional Diploma in Reading from Hofstra University. She was a teacher and reading consultant for many years, and is the author of numerous books for young readers.

For a complete listing of all Yearling titles, write to Dell Readers Service, P.O. Box 1045, South Holland, IL 60473.

George Washington Carver

AGRICULTURAL SCIENTIST

Sam and Beryl Epstein

Illustrated by Wayne Alfano

A YOUNG YEARLING BOOK

Published by
Dell Publishing
a division of
Bantam Doubleday Dell Publishing Group, Inc.
666 Fifth Avenue
New York, New York 10103

Text copyright © 1960 by Sam and Beryl Epstein

Illustrations copyright © 1991 by Wayne Alfano

All rights reserved. No part of this book may be reproduced or
transmitted in any form or by any means, electronic or mechanical,
including photocopying, recording or by any information storage
and retrieval system, without the written permission of the
Publisher, except where permitted by law.

The trademark Yearling® is registered in the U.S. Patent and
Trademark Office.
The trademark Dell® is registered in the U.S. Patent and Trademark
Office.

ISBN: 0-440-40404-5

Printed in the United States of America

January 1991

10   9   8   7   6   5   4   3   2   1
WES

Contents

1
The Stolen Baby

It was a cold night in the early days of the Civil War. A band of outlaws was riding toward the little town of Diamond Grove, Missouri.

"Night riders are coming!" From farm to farm the news was sent. "Run!" Most slaves

1

heard the warning and hid them-
selves.

But one slave, a young woman,
stayed in her small cabin on the
Carver farm. Her husband was dead.
Her little son, Jim, and her sick
baby, George, were with her. Her
owner, Farmer Carver, had not
warned her about the outlaws.
Farmer Carver thought that Mary
and her children would be safe.

He told Mrs. Carver, "The night
riders won't harm Mary and her
boys. They steal only strong men to
sell in the slave markets."

Suddenly the Carvers heard horses
galloping. The hoofbeats were loud
in the stillness of the night.

"The outlaws!" Mrs. Carver cried. "They are coming here after all!"

Farmer Carver hurried to Mary's little cabin.

"Run! Quick!" he told her. "You take George with you. I will bring Jim." He picked up the boy and hurried out with him. He thought Mary was close behind with her baby.

Farmer Carver almost reached the safety of his own house. Then he stopped. He had heard a scream and loud voices.

"Mary!" he shouted. He ran back toward the cabin.

It was too late. Mary and her sick baby had been carried off by the outlaws.

Daylight finally came. Some of the

farmers of the neighborhood got together. They decided to try to get their slaves back. First they collected all the money they could spare. "If we pay those men enough," they said, "they may let our slaves return."

Farmer Carver could not offer his friends any money. But he told them to take along his only horse. "She is worth three hundred dollars," he said. "The thieves can have her for Mary and the baby."

Almost a week passed. Then Mrs. Carver saw one of the men ride into her yard. "Where is Mary?" she cried. "Couldn't you save her?"

"No, ma'am," the man said sadly. "The outlaws agreed to take your horse for the woman and her baby.

They told us to tie the mare to a tree and go away until they signaled. They said we would find Mary and her baby in the mare's place when we came back. But they fooled us. This is all we found."

The man handed Mrs. Carver a bundle wrapped in a shawl.

Mrs. Carver unwound the shawl. "It's Mary's baby!" she cried.

The tiny body was icy cold. The eyes were closed in the little face.

"He's dead," Farmer Carver said quietly.

Just then the little body moved. A cough sounded in the sick baby's throat.

"He's not dead!" Mrs. Carver whispered. "But we must get him warm!" She hurried into the house.

Farmer Carver knew they would never see Mary again. They would miss her very much.

He sighed. Then he sighed again as he thought of his mare. He knew he would never see her again either.

It was a poor exchange, he thought. A fine horse for a tiny baby that would surely be dead before morning!

2
Young Plant Doctor

The next morning the baby was still alive. He choked on his milk. He coughed all the time. But he didn't die.

A month passed. A year went by,

and then another. Still Mary's little George was alive.

Times were hard for the Carvers. The War Between the North and the South went on and on. Soldiers trampled the Missouri fields. They took food that farmers had raised for their own families.

But finally the war ended. Farmer Carver said, "This year we will be able to keep our crop for ourselves."

Slavery had ended too.

"From now on," Mrs. Carver said, "Mary's sons are free."

Little George heard her. "What does that mean—to be free?" he asked.

Mrs. Carver looked at him. He was very small for his age. His legs and arms were thin as matchsticks. His eyes seemed too big for his little face. But those eyes were very bright and eager.

"It means you are not a slave, George," she said. "It means you can make something of yourself."

That night Farmer Carver spoke to his wife. "Jim is a strong boy," he said. "If he stays with us, I can teach him to be a good farmer. But little George will never be strong enough for farm work. It is not fair to tell him he can make something of himself."

The next morning Farmer Carver went out to plow his fields. He took Jim with him. He left George behind.

"Don't worry, George," Mrs. Carver said. "Some day you may grow bigger and stronger. Then you can work in the fields too."

George did not seem the least bit worried. "I can do some things now," he said. "I can help you."

"Of course you can," Mrs. Carver said. "Look. I will teach you to use a broom."

The broom was taller than George. But soon Mrs. Carver said, "You sweep better than I do, George!"

George grinned. "I made something of myself," he said. "I made a sweeper."

George learned to wash dishes too. He learned to make corn bread. He just watched Mrs. Carver. Then he did what she did.

He watched her plant her vegetable

garden. Then he dug up flowers and ferns in the woods and carried them home. He planted them in a secret garden of his own.

"I will take care of you," he told the plants. "Maybe if I watch carefully, I can learn what makes you grow best."

One day a neighbor said, "Your flowers are much finer than mine. Mine are dying."

"Maybe I can help them," George said.

And he did. Other people asked him to help their plants too. "You have made yourself a real plant doctor, George," they told him.

But one day George came home looking sad. "Mrs. Williams's sick

rosebush died," he told Mrs. Carver. "I carried water to it every day. I killed the tiny bugs I found on its leaves. But I couldn't save it. I don't know enough." Then he added, "I wish I could go to the school."

Mrs. Carver looked sad too.

"I know," George told her. "I know that only white children can go to school."

Mrs. Carver seemed to be thinking very hard. "There is a school for black children in Neosho," she said finally.

George's eyes got brighter than ever. "Could I go there?" he asked.

"There would be nobody to look after you in Neosho," she told him.

"I am thirteen," George said. "I could look after myself."

A few weeks later George left. He couldn't take his flowers with him. But in his pocket was his other dearest treasure. It was a handful of shiny stones he had collected.

In a bundle over his shoulder was everything else he owned. The Carvers had given him his clothes. They had given him their name too.

His mother had called him George. But slaves had no last name, and so his mother could not give him one. Now he would call himself George Washington Carver.

3

A New Aunt

George didn't know anyone in Neo-sho. He walked around until it was dark. Then he crept into a barn to sleep.

In the morning he washed in a stream. He wanted to look neat and clean. He was going to hunt for work. He had to earn enough to pay the school's small fee. He had to earn money for food too.

He walked down the road until he saw a house. He knocked at the kitchen door. A woman answered.

"Do you have any work I can do, ma'am?" he asked.

The woman saw how small he was. "I don't have any jobs for such a little boy," she said. "But I will give you some breakfast."

"Thank you." George grinned. "I would surely enjoy breakfast. But I would like to work for it, ma'am."

After he ate he washed a pile of dishes. He swept and scrubbed the floor. He fed her hens.

"I can't weed your garden today," he told the woman. "The ground is too dry. So I will water it now. Tomorrow I will weed it."

"You have certainly earned your breakfast," the woman said to George. "You have earned this too." She gave him some money. "I will tell my friends what a good worker you are."

Soon George had enough money to go to school. Every morning he sat on a bench crowded with other children. Every afternoon he hurried out to work.

Sometimes a man let George sleep in his barn. Sometimes a woman let him sleep in her cellar. Finally he found a real home. He stayed with a warmhearted African-American woman known as Aunt Maria. Her house was next to the school.

At recess George jumped the fence into her yard. He put his open book where he could see it. Then, while he read, he peeled potatoes or washed some clothes. He worked and studied until the bell called him back to class.

One day George said to Aunt Maria, "I have learned everything my teacher knows. I must find a smarter teacher in a better school."

Aunt Maria nodded. "I will miss you, George," she said. "But you must keep learning. Where will you go?"

"To Kansas," George told her. "I can ride there with some people I know, on their wagon."

Once more George put his shiny stones in his pocket. He wrapped his clean, shabby clothes in a bundle. Inside the bundle was a new treasure. It was a Bible Aunt Maria had given him.

"I will always keep it," he promised her.

4
Welcome to Simpson

Several years went by. George did not stay long in Kansas. He moved from place to place looking for better schools. He finished grade school. He began to go to high school. In every class he was the smallest and the most eager to learn.

Then suddenly George started to grow. He shot up like a beanstalk. By the time he finished high school he was six feet tall.

A friend said, "Being so tall, and knowing so much, you can get a real good job now."

"I'm tall enough," George said. "But I still don't know enough. Now I'm going to college."

"What!" the friend said. "I never heard of a Negro going to college."

George laughed. "Well," he said, "you are hearing of one now."

"But what college will take a Negro?" the friend asked.

"Highland College in Kansas,"

George told him. "I sent my school record there. And the head of the college wrote me a letter. He said any student with my high marks would be mighty welcome. I will start next term."

First George visited Aunt Maria and the Carvers. They were sad because George's brother Jim had died. But they were happy to see George. And they were very proud when he said he was going to college. There was a party for George in each house he visited.

Then he walked to Highland College. He went into the office of Dr. Brown, the head of the college.

"I am George Washington Carver,

sir," he said. "You wrote and said I could study here."

Dr. Brown stared at him. "But you're not white!" he said. "I never would have accepted you, if I had known that. We don't take blacks here!"

George couldn't say anything at all. He turned and walked away. He gave up hope of going to college. He didn't care where he went. He wandered about, moving from job to job, from town to town.

George liked best to work in gardens. He even tried to paint pictures of the flowers he loved.

But each time he painted a picture, he thought, "I wish I could learn to be a real artist." And each time he took care of flowers he thought, "I wish I knew more about them."

One day a doctor walked into the hotel kitchen where George worked. The doctor said, "My wife heard you sing in church last Sunday. She thinks you have a fine voice." Then the doctor asked George to visit his home.

"I would like to, sir," George replied.

After that he often visited the doctor and his wife. He painted pictures for them. He sang songs with them. The doctor's wife taught him how to play the piano.

"You could become a musician, George," she said.

"You could become an artist too!" the doctor said. "You should go to college, George."

Then, for the first time, George told his new friends what had happened at Highland College.

"We will find a college for you," the woman promised.

Not long afterward she told him, "You can go to Simpson College, George. It is in Iowa. They will welcome you there."

George walked the long miles to Simpson.

"My name is Carver, sir," he told the college president. "I would like to study here."

The president saw George's quiet

dignity and eager eyes. "Welcome to Simpson," he said.

George took a deep breath, and then he smiled. He was in college at last.

5
A Dream Comes True

George couldn't afford to pay for meals and a bed at Simpson. So he rented a small room. The only thing in it was an old stove.

After paying his college fees he had just ten cents left. He spent five cents for cornmeal and five cents for meat. "I'm glad I'm a good cook," he said.

Then he walked into a store. "I want to start a laundry," he said. "I need washtubs, a washboard, and an iron. But I have no money."

The store owner trusted the tall, serious young man. "Take what you need," he said. "You can pay me later."

People were very pleased with the way George washed and ironed clothes. Soon the Carver laundry was busy.

One night several of George's friends from the college came by for their clean shirts. They stopped to visit with George.

"What a fine stone collection!" one said.

"I've picked up stones since I was knee-high to a cricket," George told him. "That red stone comes from the Ozark Hills in Missouri, where I was born."

The boys enjoyed their visit with George. They didn't want to leave.

Finally George said, "You have an early class tomorrow. So have I."

On their way home one boy said, "George's chairs and tables are made of old boxes. And he has no bed. Let's get furniture for his room!"

"He's too proud to accept presents," another said. "We'll have to do it secretly."

One day a few weeks later George

opened his door. He stood staring. There was a bed in his room, and chairs, and a desk.

He never could find out where they came from. But he knew he had good friends at Simpson.

After a time his teachers said, "You have learned all we can teach you. You must go somewhere else to study now, Carver."

One said, "Go to New York and study music."

Another said, "Go to Europe and study art."

But Carver's science teacher said, "Go to a college where you can study more about plants. Then you can become a real scientist. You like to learn. A scientist always goes on learning."

"Yes," Carver said slowly. "You are right. I would rather be a scientist than anything else in the world."

Soon he told his friends that he was going to Iowa State College at Ames. That school was famous for its scientific farm. Its scientists helped farmers grow bigger and better crops.

"I will write to them," Carver's science teacher said. "I will say the college will be lucky to have you."

Iowa State College was much bigger than Simpson. But soon Carver had many friends there too.

And never before had he had a chance to learn so much. He spent days in the big laboratories and fine greenhouses. He made experiments to find out what helped plants to grow. He worked hard to discover chemicals that could cure the sick.

When he was more than thirty years old, Carver got his college degree. He was one of the best and most popular students on the campus. When he received his diploma the clapping was as loud as thunder.

Afterward the teachers shook Carver's hand.

"We need men like you," the head of the college farm said. "Will you stay here as a teacher?"

George remembered the head of Highland College. That man hadn't wanted George to join a class of white

students. Now these white teachers were asking George to join them.

George's voice was husky. "Thank you, sir," he said. "I would like to stay here."

6
"My Own People"

Carver was happier than ever. Farmers came to ask his advice about crops. Housewives came to ask him about their gardens. Often he traveled to other towns to make speeches.

But his life changed the day he got a letter from a stranger.

The stranger's name was Booker T. Washington. He was an African-American too. He was president of a small, new school for African-Americans in Alabama. It was called Tuskegee Institute.

The letter told Carver all about the school. Then it said, "You are just the man we need here. Will you come to Tuskegee and teach scientific farming?"

After Carver read the letter he went for a long walk. He wanted to think.

Finally he started back toward the college. That night he told his friends that he was going to Tuskegee.

G.W. Carver
Iowa State Univ.
Ames. Iowa

"It is a very poor school," he said. "The students are all poor too. But Booker Washington is a remarkable man. He told the students they would have to make or grow whatever they needed. So they have built their own school buildings. They made their own furniture too."

"But what would you do there, Carver?" one friend asked.

"Teach scientific farming," Carver said.

"But surely Alabama farmers know how to farm!" the friend said.

"They do know how to farm," Carver answered. "But the cotton they have grown has worn out the soil.

"So most students think that

farming is a poor way to earn their living," he added. "They want to go to Tuskegee to learn some better way.

"However, they must raise food there in order to eat," he went on. "And I can teach them how to raise really good crops. Then they can return home and teach their families and other families to grow better crops. In that way all the black farmers in Alabama may some day have better food and better lives."

One of his friends said, "I can see that you are needed at Tuskegee, Carver. But everyone here will miss you a great deal."

"I know," Carver said. "And I will miss my many friends here. But it is partly because of them that I must go to Tuskegee."

"What do you mean, Carver?" the friend asked.

Carver explained. "They shared their education with me. Now I have an education to share too. And I think I should do just what they did. I should share it with those who need it most."

His friends still begged him to stay. "No one can take your place," they said.

"I would like to stay," Carver told them. "But my place now is with my people—my own people."

7

Treasure Hunt

An old wagon took Carver from the railroad station to Tuskegee. Again he carried all he owned. He had his stones and his Bible. He had his newest treasure too. It was a shiny microscope given to him by his Iowa friends.

The wagon pulled up in front of the school.

"Welcome to Tuskegee," Dr. Washington said. He saw Carver look at the few plain buildings and the hard clay land around them.

"There is very little to work with here," he said.

"The land is poor," Carver agreed. "But fertilizer can make it rich again."

"Farmers in Alabama can't afford fertilizer," Dr. Washington said.

Carver smiled. "Then I must get to work in my laboratory here. There I'll find other ways to help the soil."

Dr. Washington led him down a

bare hall and opened a door. "This is your laboratory," he said.

The room was empty.

Carver took a deep breath. Then he set his new microscope on the floor. "There!" he said. "Now we have one thing to work with. My students and I will make the other things we need."

A few days later Carver met his new pupils. There were only thirteen of them. They looked thin and hungry. He knew it was not easy for a hungry boy to study and learn. And he knew these boys didn't like farming.

"Today," he said, "we will go on a treasure hunt for junk."

"Junk, sir?" a boy asked. For the first time the class looked interested.

"That's right," Carver said. "We will collect scraps that nobody else wants." Then he told them what to look for.

Hours later thirteen smiling boys returned. They were carrying all sorts of things—old bottles, pots and pans, some bits of string and wire, and an old oil lamp.

"Now," Carver told them, "we will make the things we need for our laboratory. We will make a little stove out of this lamp. We will make test tubes out of these little bottles. We will punch holes in this pan and make a strainer."

After several days the room looked almost like a real laboratory. The boys were very proud of it. They told

other boys that the farming class was fun. Soon Carver had more students.

"Today we are going out into the fields," Carver said one morning. "Each of you take one of these old pans."

"What for?" cried the boys.

"We want to make the soil around the school better," Carver said. "First we must find out what the soil needs. To do this we have to put some soil in each pan. Then we'll come back to the laboratory to test it. Our tests will show us what to feed the soil. We will make good fields out of poor ones."

The boys thought he was joking.

Then they remembered that he had made a laboratory out of junk.

One boy said, "I guess you can make just about anything, Professor!"

8
A School on Wheels

At spring planting time there were almost a hundred students in Carver's class. He took them all outdoors.

"This field has the poorest soil of all the ones we tested," he said. "For many years cotton was grown here.

Cotton uses up the plant food in the soil. We must make the soil rich again.

"Our job will take at least three years," he warned them. "So let's get started."

First they spread swamp mud over the field. Then they added cornstalks, garbage, and sweepings from the barn.

"There is good plant food in all of this," Carver said. "We will plow it deep into the soil. Then we will add a special plant food called nitrogen."

"But we don't have any money to buy that kind of food," a boy said.

"We won't buy it," Carver said. "We will just plant a crop of cowpeas. Cowpeas belong to a plant family called legumes. A legume can take nitrogen out of the air, through its leaves. Then it puts the nitrogen into the soil, through its roots. Cowpeas are good to eat too."

The boys turned up their noses at his last words.

Carver grinned. "They are good when I cook them," he said.

Months later they picked their crop. "It isn't very big," the boys said.

"But it has helped the soil," Carver told them. "And now we will have a feast."

He cooked cowpeas with bacon. He made cowpea pancakes. He made mashed cowpea "meat" loaf. He roasted cowpeas and made a drink

that tasted like coffee. The boys gob-
bled up everything.

"You're right!" they said. "Cowpeas
are good!"

The next year Carver and the students plowed more swamp mud into
the field. Then they planted sweet
potatoes.

"These are legumes too," Carver
said.

Finally, the third year, Carver
planted cotton in the field. The
plants grew fine and tall. The harvest
was big. Dr. Washington said, "We
will sell it and use the money for the
school."

By then many farmers around Tuskegee had heard of Carver's field.
They came to see it.

"Look!" they said. "His crop is more than three times as big as ours!"

"You can grow big crops too," Carver said. "But you must not plant cotton in the same field every year. Land needs to rest." Then he told them how to plant legumes and feed the soil. "If you do that," he said, "you can grow fine cotton in each field every three years."

"And you will have good food the other two years," one of his students said. "Just ask the professor how he cooks cowpeas. He makes them taste fine!"

Slowly the Tuskegee fields got better. Tuskegee students had more and better food. The farms nearby got better too. And the farmers' families grew healthier. But Carver wanted to help all the farmers in Alabama.

"They can't all come here," he thought. "Even if I wrote down what they should do, it won't help. Most of them can't read. I guess I'll have to go visiting."

He painted a wagon in bright colors. Then he filled it with many things. "This is our traveling school," he said.

All his students said, "We want to go with you, Professor!"

Carver smiled. "There are too many of you. You will have to take turns."

Every year the wagon made a trip through Alabama. It stopped at the

center of a village or at a farm. People came from miles around to see it. They laughed at the jokes Carver told. Then they looked at what he showed them.

"This is the kind of plow you should use," he told farmers. He showed them the new plow on his wagon.

"And here is a fine healthy cow," he said. He pointed to a cow tied behind the wagon. Then he told them how to take care of a cow so that their children could have good rich milk.

He talked to farmers' wives too. "Feed your families something besides pork and corn," he said. "Pick wild greens for salads. Grow vegetables in your yard."

Sometimes he gave them seeds or plants. He told them how to cook cowpeas and make other good cheap dishes.

He also showed the farmers' wives how to make their yards and houses prettier. He taught them to make curtains out of flour sacks. He taught them to make rugs out of grass. He showed them how to make paint out of the colored clays in Alabama soil.

"Now you can paint your houses, and it won't cost you a penny," he promised.

"Think of that!" one woman said. "I never thought I'd live in a painted house in all my life. Professor Carver is a wonderful man!"

9
Peanuts

Many farmers took Carver's advice. They learned to grow more and better cotton. Then millions of bugs called boll weevils came into Alabama. They ate the whole cotton crop.

"What can we do?" the farmers asked.

"Plant peanuts," Carver told them. "The weevils won't hurt them. Peanuts will help your soil too."

"But who would buy peanuts?" farmers asked.

"People buy peanuts at the circus," Carver pointed out. "Those peanuts come from across the ocean. Grow peanuts here and people will buy them."

"We'll try it," the farmers agreed.

That autumn the first part of the peanut crop was sold. Then peanuts began to pile up in barns and warehouses.

"Nobody wants tons of peanuts!"

the farmers cried. "We are ruined,
Carver. It is your fault!"

Carver sat alone in his room that
night. For hours he read his Bible.
He always turned to it when he was
troubled.

Suddenly he said, "I was a tiny, sickly baby once. But God found some use for me. Surely tons of peanuts must be useful too! I've only got to find the right way to use them."

He got several big bags of peanuts. Then he locked himself inside his laboratory.

Two days and nights passed. Everybody at Tuskegee was worried. "Is Carver crazy?" they asked.

Finally his laboratory door opened. Carver looked very tired, but he was smiling. "Come in," he told his friends and students.

There were rows of jars and test tubes on his tables.

"Everything that you see here has been made out of peanuts," he said.

He picked up one jar. "This is milk—peanut milk. I can make butter out of it. I can whip cream from it. I will make cheese from it when I have time."

In those two days and nights Carver had made dozens of things from peanuts. Later he made even more. All together, he made more than three hundred peanut products. Among them were paper, cardboard, face cream, sauces, dyes, and flour.

In time new factories were built to make many of those things. The factories gave jobs to hundreds of men and women. And the factories used all the peanuts that southern farmers could grow.

10
Wizard of Tuskegee

Many years later, Carver's assistant had an exciting idea. "Let's make a George Washington Carver Museum," he said.

The new president of Tuskegee agreed at once. "We can use the school's old laundry building," he said. "It will make a fine museum."

Carver smiled when he heard the news. He thought of the many shirts he had washed and ironed to earn money. This was the way he had paid his college fees. "I would like that," he said.

Carver was old now and not strong. While people were planning the museum, Carver became ill. But he wanted to get well. He wasn't going to miss the fun!

And it was fun collecting the exhibits. They found some things Carver had made out of junk for his first laboratory. They even found the skeleton of Betsy, the ox that had helped plow Carver's first fields at Tuskegee.

"We'll show the 300 things you made out of peanuts," Carver's assistant said, "and the 118 things you made out of sweet potatoes. We'll also show the wallboard and paving blocks and other things you have made out of cotton." Then he added with a grin, "No wonder the newspapers call you the Wizard of Tuskegee!"

"We must hang some of your flower paintings," a teacher said. "And we'll put your stone collection on a special shelf."

Soon the museum was ready. Carver had an office in it. There was also a small greenhouse in back where he could continue to experiment with plants.

"I have so much work left to do," Carver said.

"Now you'll have more time for your work," his assistant replied. "You won't be bothered by visitors who want to learn about the things you have made. All those things will be in the museum. People can look at them there."

However, Carver still saw many visitors. He was now famous the world over. Scientists came to exchange ideas. Farmers and factory owners came to get advice. Henry Ford, the founder of the Ford Motor Company, was one of Carver's friends.

"You have started a new science, Dr. Carver," Mr. Ford said. "You have shown people that they can make

70

new products out of ordinary plants."

Often old students came to see Carver. "I want to tell you," many of them said, "that I am trying to teach other people the things you taught me."

Carver was happy to know that his work would go on. That meant more to him than all the honors he had received.

In 1943 Carver died. Since then, more and more people have visited the Carver Museum. They say it is like a visit with Dr. Carver himself.

George Washington Carver always said, "There is a use for almost everything." The things in the Carver Museum prove he was right.